Atlantic Diet Meal Plans For Beginners

Nutrient-Rich Recipes for Healthy Living with the Atlantic Diet Plan

HARLYN RYAN

Copyright© 2024 by Harlyn Ryan

All rights reserved. Without the publisher's prior written consent, no part of this publication may be copied, distributed, or transmitted in any way, including by photocopying, recording, or other electronic or mechanical methods, with the exception of brief quotations used in critical reviews and other noncommercial uses allowed by copyright law.

TABLE OF CONTENT

PREFACE 7

CHAPTER ONE 11

  Origin and Overview of Atlantic Diet 11

    Health Benefits of Atlantic Diets 13

    Pros of the Atlantic Diet 15

    Cons of the Atlantic Diet 16

    Tips for Starting the Atlantic Diet 17

CHAPTER TWO 19

  Breakfast Recipes 19

    Savory Spinach and Feta Omelette 20

    Blueberry and Almond Overnight Oats 22

    Smoked Salmon and Avocado Toast 23

    Mushroom and Spinach Breakfast Burrito 25

    Greek Yogurt Parfait with Fresh Fruit 27

CHAPTER THREE 29

  Lunch Recipes 29

    Quinoa Salad with Roasted Vegetables 30

    Tuna Salad Stuffed Avocado 32

Grilled Shrimp and Vegetable Skewers 33

Tomato and Basil Bruschetta 35

Atlantic Fish Tacos with Cabbage Slaw 37

CHAPTER FOUR 41

Dinner Recipes 41

Grilled Lemon Herb Chicken 42

Baked Cod with Garlic and Herbs 43

Lentil and Vegetable Stew 45

Mediterranean Chickpea Salad 48

Roasted Vegetable and Goat Cheese Tart 50

CHAPTER FIVE 55

Snack and Appetizer Recipes 55

Hummus and Crudites Platter 56

Stuffed Grape Leaves with Tzatziki Sauce 57

Spiced Nuts and Seeds Mix 59

Marinated Olives and Feta Cheese 61

Baked Sweet Potato Chips with Herbed Yogurt Dip 63

CHAPTER SIX 67

Soup Recipes 67

Classic Portuguese Caldo Verde Soup 68

Creamy Tomato and Red Pepper Soup 70

Italian Minestrone Soup 74

Clam Chowder with Fresh Herbs 76

CHAPTER SEVEN 79

Pasta and Grain Recipes 79

Mediterranean Orzo Salad 80

Pesto Pasta with Cherry Tomatoes 82

Spaghetti Squash with Tomato Basil Sauce 84

Barley Risotto with Mushrooms and Parmesan 86

Farro Salad with Roasted Vegetables 88

CHAPTER EIGHT 91

Seafood Recipes 91

Grilled Swordfish with Lemon and Herbs 92

Pan-Seared Scallops with Citrus Salsa 94

Baked Salmon with Dill and Lemon 96

Shrimp and Vegetable Stir-Fry 97

Tuna Nicoise Salad 100

CHAPTER NINE 103

Vegetable Side Dish Recipes 103

Roasted Garlic Cauliflower Mash 104

    Sauteed Green Beans with Almonds 106

    Balsamic Glazed Brussels Sprouts 107

    Grilled Asparagus with Lemon Zest 109

    Sauteed Swiss Chard with Garlic and Lemon 111

CHAPTER TEN **115**

  Dessert Recipes 115

    Fresh Fruit Salad with Honey Lime Dressing 116

    Greek Yogurt with Honey and Walnuts 117

    Orange and Almond Cake 119

    Berry Compote with Vanilla Greek Yogurt 121

    Chocolate Avocado Mousse 123

CHAPTER ELEVEN **125**

  Beverage Recipes 125

    Iced Green Tea with Mint 125

    Citrus Infused Water 127

    Smoothie with Spinach, Pineapple, and Coconut Water 128

    Lemon Ginger Detox Drink 130

    Turmeric Latte with Almond Milk 131

CHAPTER TWELVE **133**

  Conclusion 133

PREFACE

Recall the initial taste of an exquisite meal. The wave of contentment, the pleasant warmth, and the explosion of taste. Imagine having that sensation every day—a delightful tapestry of healthful decisions that feed your body and spirit—rather than just once. The Atlantic Diet holds this promise, and this cookbook will help you create your own culinary symphony.

However, let's face it—going on a new diet might be scary. You're faced with a deluge of contradictory data, onerous regulations, and the anxiety of flavorless, boring food. Everybody has been there, gazing at a refrigerator brimming with "shoulds" rather than mouthwatering options.

What if I told you that the goal of the Atlantic Diet is liberation rather than restriction? It's about rediscovering the power of using the abundance of nature to fuel your body, the joy of cooking, and the bright flavors of genuine food.

My personal desire for wellness led me to embark on the Atlantic Diet, rather than following a doctor's advice. Stress and years of processed food have taken their toll. I felt unsteady, unconnected to my body, and lethargic. I yearned for a shift, for a means to feel alive and energetic once more.

That's when I came across the Atlantic Diet. It was a balanced approach with an emphasis on entire, fresh foods from both the land and the sea rather than a fad diet. It satisfied my needs for flavor, sustainability, and simplicity. I set out on this new gastronomic journey cautiously optimistic.

And it was a revelation, I tell you. The meals were orchestras of flavor rather than tasteless constraints. Imagine delicate fish that has been coated with herbs and lemon, the flavor dancing on your tongue. Imagine colorful bowls of quinoa filled to overflowing with roasted veggies and smooth avocado, where every mouthful is an ode to the abundance of nature. My taste buds and eyes were opened to a world of possibilities by the Atlantic Diet, where tasty and healthy could coexist peacefully instead of being mutually exclusive.

It was more than a culinary adventure, though. The idea was to rediscover the kitchen as a creative and nourishing retreat. Every chopped vegetable and every sizzling in the pan turned into a mindful cooking activity that helped me stay in the present and practice self-care.

The truth is, neither a nutritionist nor a skilled cook am I. I'm just an ordinary person who came to understand the life-changing potential of eating well. And that journey is reflected in this cookbook. It's not a compilation of difficult-to-follow recipes. It is a veritable gold mine of mouthwatering, simple-to-make recipes that honor real food, real taste, and the real you.

Anyone looking for a lively, well-rounded attitude to life should read this book. These recipes are an invitation to join the symphony, whether you're an experienced chef or a culinary novice, health-conscious or just craving good food.

Recall that this is more than simply a cookbook as you page through the pages. It's a manual for discovering the joy of eating healthily, lovingly caring for your body, and unleashing your own creative cooking potential. So let's get cooking, throw on your apron, and turn on the music!

CHAPTER ONE

Origin and Overview of Atlantic Diet

Scholars have dubbed the customary dietary regimen found in northwest Portugal and Spain the "Atlantic diet." Despite their shared characteristics, Dr. Calvo-Malvar claims that there are some notable differences between the diet and the Mediterranean diet.

Similar to the Mediterranean diet, the Atlantic diet emphasizes the consumption of fresh, in-season, and locally sourced foods like fruits, vegetables, cereals, pulses (dry beans, lentils, and chickpeas), seafood, dairy products, and olive oil for dressing and cooking. But according to Calvo-Malvar, the Atlantic diet often has higher proportions of fish, dairy, potatoes, fruits, and vegetables than the Mediterranean diet does.

The Spanish Nutrition Foundation (FEN), University of Santiago de Compostela, Instituto Polit-ecnico de Viana do Castelo (IPVC), and Galician Association for the study of the Atlantic Diet (ASGAEDA) came together a few years ago to create the Atlantic Diet concept. Their goal was to establish the Atlantic Diet as a global standard for a healthful diet. The European Center for the Atlantic Diet (CEDA) was established in Portugal in 2003 as a consequence of talks between experts from the Spanish and Portuguese Atlantic areas.

Consequently, the University of Santiago de Compostela in Galicia, Spain established the "Atlantic Diet Foundation" in 2007.

These institutions and groups that support the Atlantic Diet signed the "Baione Declaration on the Atlantic Diet" in 2006 with the intention of creating a plan for the promotion and upkeep of the diet at various levels, with the following goals in mind:

- The promotion of the Atlantic Diet as a source of health and pleasure;
- The promotion of research, development and innovation on the Atlantic Diet, with respect to health in the area of fisheries, aquaculture, agriculture, livestock, viticulture and natural resources;
- The development and use of the key components of the Atlantic Diet within primary and supplemental foods, through both conventional and creative cooking preparations and supply for consumption at home and outside of it, by the food business, tourist, and catering sectors;
- The involvement of the educational sector at various levels to educate consumers about the cultural heritage of the Atlantic Diet;
- Ensure that public and private institutions recognize the values of the Atlantic diet, lifestyle and the accompanying

environmental commitments, and are committed to their protection and promotion as a functional diet;
- Evaluate how upholding the principles of the Atlantic Diet might affect the environment in the widest sense (urbanization, transportation, pollution, etc.).

Health Benefits of Atlantic Diets

The Atlantic Diet is becoming more well-known for its many health advantages. It is based on the culinary customs of nations that border the Atlantic Ocean, primarily Portugal and Galicia in Spain. The abundance of the ocean and the surrounding landscapes serve as inspiration for this diet, which places a strong emphasis on seasonal, local, and fresh foods.

Starchy foods like bread, pasta, rice, cereals, and other whole grains make up the majority of an Atlantic diet. The diet also contained eggs and meat, primarily pork and beef. At mealtimes, wine is drank in moderation and olive oil is another popular condiment.

A recent Spanish study involving 250 families found that eating an Atlantic diet significantly reduced the incidence of stroke, diabetes, and high blood pressure. These are some of its health advantages:

Abundance of Nutrient-Rich Seafood: Eating seafood that is high in nutrients is a key component of the Atlantic Diet. Omega-3 fatty acids are abundant in fish, including sardines, mackerel, and salmon, and they are crucial for heart health, cognitive function, and the reduction of inflammation.

Heart-Healthy Monounsaturated Fats: An essential component of the Atlantic diet, olive oil contains monounsaturated fats that have been connected to better cardiovascular health. These fats help lower blood levels of harmful cholesterol and lower the risk of heart disease.

Antioxidant-Rich Fruits and Vegetables: A wide range of fruits and vegetables, including leafy greens, tomatoes, and peppers, are highly valued in the diet. These vibrant offerings are bursting with antioxidants that enhance general health and shield cells from harm.

Whole Grains for Sustained Energy: Complex carbohydrates included in whole grains like quinoa, brown rice, and oats provide you long-lasting energy and support healthy digestion. They also help regulate weight by enhancing feelings of fullness.

Moderate Consumption of Dairy: Dairy products are allowed in moderation, especially yoghurt and cheese. These products support bone health and a balanced gut flora by supplying vital nutrients like probiotics and calcium.

Emphasis on Local and Seasonal Produce: The Atlantic Diet promotes the use of seasonal and regionally obtained foods to maximize nutritional value and ensure freshness. This strategy benefits nearby communities and is consistent with sustainable principles.

Reduced Processed Foods and Added Sugars: The Atlantic Diet's low dependence on processed foods and added sugars is one of its defining characteristics. This helps control weight and lowers the chance of chronic illnesses linked to a diet heavy in processed foods and sweets.

The Atlantic Diet is unique in that it combines the greatest aspects of local cuisines from all over the Atlantic Ocean to nourish the body holistically. A balanced lifestyle and a focus on fresh, nutrient-rich foods can help adherents of the Atlantic Diet reap a host of health benefits, including better digestion and heart health. For a tasty and nutritious experience, think about adding components of this diet to your cooking endeavors.

Pros of the Atlantic Diet

According to Yawitz, the Atlantic diet is high in antioxidants, vitamins, minerals, fiber, and good fats and low in saturated fat. According to her, there were notable changes in waist circumference and HDL (good) cholesterol in the 574 patients in the 2024 trial who followed the diet for six months.

Yawitz notes other new research that indicates the Atlantic diet may help lower depression and increase longevity.

The Atlantic diet emphasizes seafood and good fats like those in fish and olive oil, which Routhenstein finds appealing. This may lower the chance of developing cardiovascular problems and enhance heart health.

People who ate more than half a teaspoon of olive oil daily had reduced odds of cardiovascular disease-related premature death than those who never or seldom used the oil, based on a 2022 study that was written up in the American College of Cardiology's Journal. Because extra virgin olive oil contains a lot of antioxidants including oleocanthal, which is known to help reduce inflammation, dietitians praise it as a healthy fat. (The fact that chronic inflammation is associated with a number of illnesses, such as diabetes, cancer, heart disease, and more, makes it a major worry.)

According to dietitian Michelle Saari, R.D.N. of EHealth Project, the health benefits of the Atlantic diet are similar to those of the Mediterranean diet in that they are generally beneficial for long-term cognitive function. Omega-3 fats are abundant in fresh seafood and olive oil, and they are connected to improved brain function.

Cons of the Atlantic Diet

Although the previously mentioned studies show promise, there hasn't been much research done on the Atlantic diet, according to Yawitz. Considering that Southern Europeans have been eating this manner for millennia, this is startling.

"Based on the research that is now available and considering its resemblance to the Mediterranean diet, the diet appears to be generally quite healthful," she states. Having said that, the plan differs from the Mediterranean diet just enough to merit additional research."

According to Routhenstein, people who reside in areas with restricted access to fresh seafood may encounter difficulties adhering to the diet. Furthermore, the Atlantic diet strongly promotes cooking from scratch, which may be difficult for certain people to do on a regular basis, according to Saari.

Tips for Starting the Atlantic Diet

Although adopting a new diet can be daunting, you can gradually adapt to the Atlantic diet by making little adjustments to your present eating habits.

For instance, Yawitz recommends switching from white bread to whole grain bread, grilling fish instead of strip steak, or ordering vegetable soup in place of broccoli cheddar.

There aren't many recipe books at your neighborhood bookstore for the Atlantic diet because it's still a relatively new diet trend, the expert adds. In case you need inspiration, you can browse cookbooks featuring Mediterranean diets or conduct an internet search for nutritious meals in Spanish or Portuguese.

According to Saari, here are a few more pointers for beginning the Atlantic diet:

Start with seafood: A few times a week, try include fish or shellfish in your meals. Seek out locally available fresh and sustainable options. Seafood that has been frozen still has nutrients in it.

Increase plant-based foods: Increase the amount of whole grains, fruits, and vegetables in your diet. Your health will improve if you eat half a plate of fruits and vegetables at every meal. Try experimenting with nuts and legumes as meal or snack options.

Use olive oil: Olive oil can be used in place of other fats in dressings and cooking.

Eat dairy and meat in moderation: Reduce your intake of dairy and red meat and emphasize more plant-based foods in your diet.

CHAPTER TWO

Breakfast Recipes

The Atlantic Diet emphasizes starting your day with nutritious and satisfying meals that provide sustained energy throughout the morning. This chapter offers a variety of delicious and balanced breakfast options rich in whole grains, lean protein, healthy fats, and essential vitamins and minerals.

Here are some key principles for Atlantic Diet breakfasts:

Focus on whole foods: Opt for fresh fruits, vegetables, whole grains, nuts, seeds, and lean protein sources.

Limit processed foods: Avoid sugary cereals, pastries, and breakfast meats.

Include healthy fats: Incorporate nuts, seeds, avocado, or olive oil for satiety and nutrient absorption.

Balance your plate: Aim for a combination of carbohydrates, protein, and healthy fats for sustained energy.

Now, let's explore some delicious breakfast recipes that embrace these principles:

Savory Spinach and Feta Omelette

Prep Time: 5 minutes

Cook Time: 10 minutes

Servings: 1

Ingredients:

2 large eggs

1 tablespoon milk (optional)

1/4 teaspoon salt

1/4 teaspoon black pepper

1 tablespoon olive oil

1 cup chopped fresh spinach

2 tablespoons crumbled feta cheese

Directions:

Mix the eggs, milk, pepper, and salt in a bowl.

In a nonstick pan, warm the olive oil over medium heat.

Cook the spinach for one minute, or until it has wilted.

Swirl to coat the bottom of the pan as you pour the egg mixture in.

Using a spatula, carefully lift the omelette's edges as it cooks to allow the raw egg to flow below.

Over one half of the omelette, scatter feta cheese.

Over the cheese, fold the remaining half.

Cook for an additional minute or two, or until cooked to your preference.

Enjoy and serve right now!

Tips:

For more taste and nutrients, add other chopped veggies, like as peppers, onions, or mushrooms.

For added flavor, use finely chopped fresh herbs like dill or parsley.

Accompany with sliced fruit or whole-wheat bread.

Nutritional Values (per serving):

Calories: 280

Fat: 14g

Carbohydrates: 10g

Protein: 18g

Blueberry and Almond Overnight Oats

Prep Time: 5 minutes

Total Time: (Ovkiernight)

Servings: 1

Ingredients:

1/2 cup rolled oats

1/2 cup unsweetened almond milk

1/4 cup plain Greek yogurt

1/4 cup fresh or frozen blueberries

1 tablespoon sliced almonds

1/4 teaspoon ground cinnamon (optional)

Directions:

Oats, almond milk, yogurt, blueberries, almonds, and cinnamon (if using) should all be combined in a jar or other container.

Stir well, cover, and refrigerate overnight.

Stir once more in the morning and serve cold or slightly heated.

Tips:

For additional taste and texture, top with chopped nuts, chia seeds, or a drizzle of honey.

For variation, use several kinds of fruits or berries.

Prepare a bigger quantity and divide it into portions for quick breakfasts all week long.

Nutritional Values (per serving):

Calories: 300

Fat: 8g

Carbohydrates: 35g

Protein: 10g

Smoked Salmon and Avocado Toast

Prep Time: 5 minutes

Cook Time: 0 minutes (optional)

Servings: 1

Ingredients:

1 slice whole-wheat bread, toasted

1/2 ripe avocado, mashed

2 ounces smoked salmon, thinly sliced

1 tablespoon lemon juice (optional)

To taste, add a pinch of salt and black pepper.

Optional garnishes: sliced red onion, capers, fresh dill

Directions:

Toast the bread until it reaches the desired doneness.

Over the toast, equally distribute the mashed avocado.

Place the pieces of smoked salmon on top of the avocado.

If desired, drizzle with lemon juice and add salt and pepper to taste.

Add optional garnishes like as fresh dill, capers, and chopped red onion.

Tips:

For a warm twist, toast the bread and briefly warm the smoked salmon in a pan before assembling.

Use mashed vegetables like cherry tomatoes or cucumber instead of avocado for a slightly different flavor profile.

Select premium smoked salmon for optimal flavor and texture.

Nutritional Values (per serving):

Calories: 350

Fat: 18g

Carbohydrates: 25g

Protein: 15g

Mushroom and Spinach Breakfast Burrito

Prep Time: 10 minutes

Cook Time: 15 minutes

Servings: 1

Ingredients:

1 whole-wheat tortilla

1 tablespoon olive oil

1/2 cup chopped mushrooms

1/4 cup chopped spinach

1/4 cup crumbled feta cheese

1 egg, scrambled

Salt and pepper, to taste

Optional garnishes: salsa, avocado slices, hot sauce

Directions:

Heat the olive oil in a pan over medium heat.

Simmer the mushrooms for five minutes or until they become tender.

Cook the spinach for one minute, or until it has wilted.

Season with salt and pepper, to taste.

The egg should be scrambled in another pan.

For a few seconds, reheat the tortilla in a dry pan or the microwave.

Cover the tortilla with the scrambled egg.

Add the cooked spinach and mushroom mixture over top.

Add some feta cheese on top.

Tightly roll the tortilla by folding the bottom and sides inward.

Serve right away with the chosen toppings.

Tips:

To add even more taste and nutrients, add finely sliced onions, peppers, or tomatoes.

For a plant-based variation, use a vegan cheese substitute.

For a full breakfast, serve with yogurt or fruit on the side.

Nutritional Values (per serving):

Calories: 380

Fat: 15g

Carbohydrates: 30g

Protein: 20g

Greek Yogurt Parfait with Fresh Fruit

Prep Time: 5 minutes

Cook Time: 0 minutes

Servings: 1

Ingredients:

1/2 cup plain Greek yogurt

1/4 cup granola

1/4 cup mixed fresh berries

1 tablespoon chopped nuts (optional)

1 tablespoon honey (optional)

Directions:

Layer the yogurt, granola, and berries in a parfait glass or bowl.

Top with chopped nuts and a drizzle of honey (optional).

Tips:

Use different types of fruits like sliced banana, mango, or pineapple for variety.

Add a sprinkle of chia seeds or hemp seeds for extra nutrients.

Make a larger batch and portion it out for quick and easy breakfasts throughout the week.

Nutritional Values (per serving):

Calories: 300

Fat: 8g

Carbohydrates: 35g

Protein: 15g

CHAPTER THREE

Lunch Recipes

The Atlantic Diet emphasizes balanced and satisfying lunches that provide sustained energy throughout the afternoon. This chapter offers a variety of delicious and portable options that are rich in protein, healthy fats, and complex carbohydrates, keeping you feeling full and focused.

Here are some key principles for Atlantic Diet lunches:

Focus on whole foods: Choose fresh ingredients like vegetables, fruits, whole grains, lean protein sources, and healthy fats.

Prioritize portion control: Aim for moderate portions to avoid overeating and maintain energy levels.

Pack variety: Include different colors and textures to keep your lunches interesting and ensure you're getting a range of nutrients.

Make it convenient: Opt for easy-to-prepare or assemble meals that fit your busy schedule.

Now, let's explore some delicious lunch recipes that embrace these principles:

Quinoa Salad with Roasted Vegetables

Prep Time: 15 minutes

Cook Time: 30 minutes

Servings: 4

Ingredients:

1 cup quinoa, rinsed

1 1/2 cups vegetable broth

1 tablespoon olive oil

1/2 teaspoon salt

1/4 teaspoon black pepper

1 cup assorted vegetables (e.g., broccoli florets, bell peppers, zucchini), chopped

1/4 cup crumbled feta cheese (optional)

2 tablespoons chopped fresh parsley

Directions:

Turn the oven on to 400°F, or 200°C.

Add one tablespoon of olive oil, salt, and pepper to chopped vegetables and toss. Place onto a baking sheet and roast for twenty to twenty-five minutes, or until crisp-tender.

Meanwhile, put the vegetable broth, rinsed quinoa, and the last 1/4 teaspoon of salt in a pot. After bringing to a boil, lower the heat, cover, and simmer the quinoa for fifteen minutes, or until it is tender and fluffy.

After cooking, use a fork to fluff the quinoa and allow it to cool slightly.

The cooked quinoa, roasted veggies, chopped parsley, and feta cheese (if using) should all be combined in a big bowl.

Serve cold or room temperature after tossing to coat.

Tips:

Use leftover roasted vegetables from another meal for a quick and easy lunch option.

Add other protein sources like grilled chicken or shrimp for a more complete meal.

Drizzle with a simple vinaigrette dressing for added flavor.

Nutritional Values (per serving):

Calories: 350

Fat: 10g

Carbohydrates: 45g

Protein: 10g

Tuna Salad Stuffed Avocado

Prep Time: 10 minutes

Cook Time: 0 minutes

Servings: 1

Ingredients:

1 ripe avocado, halved and pitted

1 can (5 oz) tuna, drained

1 tablespoon mayonnaise (or Greek yogurt for a lighter option)

1 tablespoon chopped celery

1/4 teaspoon red onion, finely chopped

1 tablespoon lemon juice

Salt and pepper to taste

Directions:

Mash the avocado flesh in a bowl with a fork, leaving some chunks.

Add drained tuna, mayonnaise, celery, red onion, lemon juice, salt, and pepper.

Mix well and fill the avocado halves with the tuna salad mixture.

Tips:

Add chopped fresh herbs like dill or parsley for extra flavor.

Serve with a side salad or whole-wheat crackers for a complete meal.

Use canned salmon or cooked shredded chicken for a variation.

Nutritional Values (per serving):

Calories: 350

Fat: 20g

Carbohydrates: 15g

Protein: 20g

Grilled Shrimp and Vegetable Skewers

Prep Time: 10 minutes

Cook Time: 10-12 minutes

Servings: 1

Ingredients:

4-5 large shrimp, peeled and deveined

1/2 red bell pepper, cut into chunks

1/2 yellow squash, cut into chunks

1/4 red onion, cut into wedges

1 tablespoon olive oil

1/2 teaspoon dried oregano

1/4 teaspoon salt

1/4 teaspoon black pepper

Lemon wedges, for serving

Directions:

Elevate the temperature of the grill or grill pan to medium-high.

Combine the shrimp, veggies, olive oil, oregano, salt, and pepper in a bowl.

Alternating between shrimp and veggies, thread the contents onto skewers.

Grill the vegetables for 5 to 6 minutes on each side, or until they are crisp-tender and the shrimp are cooked through.

Serve right away with wedges of lemon.

Tips:

Use wooden skewers and soak them in water for at least 30 minutes before grilling to prevent burning.

Marinate the shrimp and vegetables for 15-30 minutes in your favorite marinade for added flavor.

Substitute other vegetables like zucchini, mushrooms, or cherry tomatoes.

Nutritional Values (per serving):

Calories: 300

Fat: 15g

Carbohydrates: 10g

Protein: 25g

Tomato and Basil Bruschetta

Prep Time: 10 minutes

Cook Time: 0 minutes

Servings: 1

Ingredients:

1 slice whole-wheat bread, toasted

1/2 ripe tomato, diced

1 tablespoon chopped fresh basil

1 tablespoon olive oil

Balsamic glaze (optional)

Salt and pepper to taste

Directions:

Toast the bread until it reaches the desired doneness.

Apply a clove of garlic to the toasted bread (optional).

Pour some olive oil over it.

Add chopped basil, diced tomato, salt, and pepper on top.

Serve right away after adding an optional balsamic glaze drizzle.

Tips:

Use different types of bread like sourdough or rye for variety.

Add a sprinkle of crumbled feta cheese for extra flavor and protein.

Grill the tomato slices for a smoky flavor twist.

Nutritional Values (per serving):

Calories: 200

Fat: 10g

Carbohydrates: 20g

Protein: 5g

Atlantic Fish Tacos with Cabbage Slaw

Prep Time: 15 minutes

Cook Time: 10 minutes

Servings: 1

Ingredients:

4 ounces cod or another white fish fillet

1 tablespoon olive oil

1/2 teaspoon chili powder

1/4 teaspoon smoked paprika

Salt and pepper to taste

2 corn tortillas, warmed

1/4 cup shredded cabbage

1 tablespoon chopped red onion

1 tablespoon chopped cilantro

Lime wedges, for serving

Optional toppings: salsa, avocado slices, hot sauce

Directions:

Olive oil, salt, pepper, paprika, and chili powder are used to season the fish fillet.

Over medium heat, preheat a skillet or grill pan.

Fry the fish for 4–5 minutes on each side, or until it is flaky and cooked through.

Make the slaw by combining shredded cabbage, red onion, and cilantro in a bowl while the fish cooks.

Follow the directions on the package to reheat the corn tortillas.

Place the cooked fish on a hot tortilla, flaking it.

Add the desired extra toppings, lime wedges, and cabbage slaw on top.

Tips:

Use leftover cooked fish for a quick and easy lunch option.

Substitute other types of fish like salmon or mahi-mahi.

Add a dollop of Greek yogurt or sour cream for extra creaminess.

Nutritional Values (per serving):

Calories: 350

Fat: 15g

Carbohydrates: 30g

Protein: 20g

CHAPTER FOUR

Dinner Recipes

The Atlantic Diet emphasizes creating balanced and satisfying dinners that nourish your body and promote well-being. This chapter offers a variety of delicious and wholesome recipes featuring fresh, seasonal ingredients, lean protein sources, and healthy fats.

Here are some key principles for Atlantic Diet dinners:

Focus on variety: Include a diverse range of vegetables, whole grains, and lean protein sources to ensure a well-rounded nutrient intake.

Practice mindful cooking: Savor the process of preparing your meals and enjoy them slowly and without distractions.

Portion control: Aim for moderate portions to avoid overeating and maintain a healthy weight.

Embrace leftovers: Plan meals with leftovers in mind for convenient lunches or quick weeknight dinners.

Now, let's explore some delicious dinner recipes that embrace these principles:

Grilled Lemon Herb Chicken

Prep Time: 10 minutes

Cook Time: 20-25 minutes

Servings: 2

Ingredients:

2 boneless, skinless chicken breasts

1 tablespoon olive oil

1 tablespoon lemon juice

1/2 teaspoon dried oregano

1/4 teaspoon garlic powder

1/4 teaspoon salt

1/4 teaspoon black pepper

Lemon wedges, for serving (optional)

Directions:

Turn the heat up to medium-high on the grill or grill pan.

Mix the olive oil, lemon juice, oregano, garlic powder, salt, and pepper in a bowl.

Give the chicken breasts at least 15 minutes to marinate in the marinade.

Grill chicken until cooked through and the juices run clear, about 5 to 7 minutes per side.

Accompany the dish right away with optional lemon slices.

Tips:

Use boneless, skinless chicken thighs for a more flavorful option.

Add other herbs like thyme or rosemary to the marinade for additional flavor variations.

Serve with grilled vegetables or a side salad for a complete meal.

Nutritional Values (per serving):

Calories: 300

Fat: 10g

Carbohydrates: 0g

Protein: 40g

Baked Cod with Garlic and Herbs

Prep Time: 10 minutes

Cook Time: 15-20 minutes

Servings: 2

Ingredients:

2 cod fillets

1 tablespoon olive oil

1 tablespoon chopped fresh parsley

1 tablespoon chopped fresh dill

1/2 teaspoon garlic powder

1/4 teaspoon salt

1/4 teaspoon black pepper

Lemon wedges, for serving

Directions:

Preheat oven to 400°F (200°C).

Grease a baking dish very lightly.

Olive oil, parsley, dill, garlic powder, salt, and pepper should all be combined in a small bowl.

After arranging the cod fillets in the baking dish, brush them with the herb mixture.

Fish should be easily pierced with a fork after baking for 15 to 20 minutes.

Serve right away with wedges of lemon.

Tips:

Substitute other white fish like halibut or tilapia for cod.

Add chopped cherry tomatoes or sliced zucchini to the baking dish for additional flavor and vegetables.

For a full meal, serve with quinoa or brown rice.

Nutritional Values (per serving):

Calories: 350

Fat: 15g

Carbohydrates: 5g

Protein: 40g

Lentil and Vegetable Stew

Prep Time: 15 minutes

Cook Time: 40-45 minutes

Servings: 4-6

Ingredients:

1 tablespoon olive oil

1 onion, chopped

2 carrots, chopped

2 celery stalks, chopped

2 cloves garlic, minced

1 cup brown lentils, rinsed

4 cups vegetable broth

1 (14.5 oz) can diced tomatoes, undrained

1 cup chopped broccoli florets

1/2 teaspoon dried thyme

1/4 teaspoon salt

1/4 teaspoon black pepper

Chopped fresh parsley, for garnish (optional)

Directions:

In a big pot or Dutch oven, warm up the olive oil over medium heat.

Stir in the onion, carrots, and celery and simmer for about 5 minutes, or until softened.

Cook the garlic for one more minute, or until aromatic.

Add the broccoli, diced tomatoes, lentils, vegetable broth, thyme, and salt and pepper to taste.

After bringing to a boil, lower the heat, cover, and simmer the lentils for 30 to 35 minutes, or until they become soft.

If stew is too thick, stir with more broth or water.

As necessary, taste and adjust the seasonings.

Serve hot, garnished with finely chopped fresh parsley.

Tips:

Add other vegetables like chopped zucchini, green beans, or spinach for additional variety and nutrients.

Use pre-cooked lentils to reduce cooking time by about 20 minutes.

Serve with whole-wheat bread on the side for a filling and pleasant supper.

Nutritional Values (per serving):

Calories: 300

Fat: 5g

Carbohydrates: 40g

Protein: 15g

Mediterranean Chickpea Salad

Prep Time: 15 minutes

Cook Time: 0 minutes

Servings: 2

Ingredients:

1 (15 oz) can chickpeas, drained and rinsed

1/4 cup chopped cucumber

1/4 cup chopped red onion

1/4 cup chopped cherry tomatoes

1 tablespoon crumbled feta cheese

1 tablespoon chopped fresh parsley

1 tablespoon olive oil

1 tablespoon lemon juice

1/4 teaspoon dried oregano

Salt and pepper to taste

Directions:

Chickpeas, cucumber, red onion, cherry tomatoes, feta cheese, and parsley should all be combined in a bowl.

Mix the olive oil, lemon juice, oregano, salt, and pepper in a another bowl.

Drizzle the chickpea mixture with the dressing and toss to coat.

For best flavor, serve right away or refrigerate for at least half an hour.

Tips:

Use chopped bell peppers, olives, or artichoke hearts for additional flavor and texture variations.

Serve the salad on a bed of romaine lettuce or spinach for a more complete meal.

Substitute crumbled goat cheese or vegan cheese alternatives for feta cheese.

Nutritional Values (per serving):

Calories: 300

Fat: 10g

Carbohydrates: 30g

Protein: 15g

Roasted Vegetable and Goat Cheese Tart

Prep Time: 20 minutes

Cook Time: 40-45 minutes

Servings: 4-6

Ingredients:

For the crust:

1 1/4 cups all-purpose flour

1/2 teaspoon salt

1/2 cup cold unsalted butter, cubed

3-4 tablespoons ice water

For the filling:

1 tablespoon olive oil

1 onion, thinly sliced

2 zucchini, thinly sliced

1 yellow squash, thinly sliced

1 red bell pepper, thinly sliced

1/4 cup crumbled goat cheese

2 eggs, beaten

1/4 cup milk

1/4 cup grated Parmesan cheese

1/4 teaspoon dried thyme

Salt and pepper to taste

Directions:

1. Prepare the crust:

- In a bowl, whisk together flour and salt.
- Using a pastry cutter or your fingertips, cut the cold butter into the flour mixture until it resembles coarse crumbs.
- Gradually add ice water, 1 tablespoon at a time, until the dough comes together and forms a ball. Avoid overworking the dough.
- Refrigerate the dough for a minimum of half an hour after wrapping it in plastic wrap.

2. Prepare the filling:

- Preheat oven to 400°F (200°C).
- In a skillet over medium heat, warm the olive oil.
- Add onion and cook until softened, about 5 minutes.

- Add zucchini, yellow squash, and red bell pepper and cook for an additional 5-7 minutes, or until tender-crisp.
- Season with salt and pepper to taste.

3. Assemble and bake the tart:

- On a lightly floured surface, roll out the chilled dough to a 12-inch circle.
- Transfer the dough to a pie dish and gently press into the bottom and sides.
- Spread the roasted vegetables evenly over the bottom of the crust.
- In a bowl, whisk together eggs, milk, Parmesan cheese, thyme, salt, and pepper.
- Pour the egg mixture over the vegetables.
- Sprinkle crumbled goat cheese on top
- Sprinkle crumbled goat cheese on top.
- Bake for 40-45 minutes, or until the crust is golden brown and the filling is set.
- Let cool slightly before slicing and serving.

Tips:

Use a store-bought pie crust to save time.

For a vegan option, omit the goat cheese and use vegan cheese alternatives.

For a full supper, serve the tart with a side salad.

Nutritional Values (per serving):

Calories: 400

Fat: 20g

Carbohydrates: 35g

Protein: 15g

CHAPTER FIVE

Snack and Appetizer Recipes

The Atlantic Diet encourages mindful snacking and enjoying healthy appetizers that satisfy hunger without compromising your dietary goals. This chapter offers a variety of delicious and nutritious options featuring whole foods, fresh ingredients, and healthy fats.

Here are some key principles for Atlantic Diet snacks and appetizers:

Focus on nutrient density: Choose options rich in fiber, protein, healthy fats, and essential vitamins and minerals.

Portion control: Practice mindful eating and enjoy smaller portions to avoid overindulging.

Balance is key: Combine different food groups like fruits, vegetables, whole grains, and lean protein for sustained energy and satisfaction.

Make it easy and convenient: Opt for pre-prepared or easy-to-assemble options for busy schedules.

Now, let's explore some delicious snack and appetizer recipes that embrace these principles:

Hummus and Crudites Platter

Prep Time: 10 minutes

Total Time: 10 minutes

Servings: 4-6

Ingredients:

1 cup hummus (store-bought or homemade)

Assorted crudités (e.g., carrot sticks, cucumber slices, bell pepper strips, celery sticks, cherry tomatoes, broccoli florets)

Optional additions: pita bread, crackers, olives, marinated artichoke hearts

Directions:

Arrange the hummus in a serving bowl.

Wash and prepare the crudités, arranging them around the hummus on a platter.

Include any additional desired items like pita bread, crackers, olives, or marinated artichoke hearts.

Tips:

Choose colorful and seasonal vegetables for variety and visual appeal.

For a protein boost, add slices of roasted chickpeas or crumbled feta cheese.

Drizzle the hummus with olive oil and a sprinkle of paprika for extra flavor.

Nutritional Values (per serving with hummus and assorted vegetables):

Calories: 200

Fat: 10g

Carbohydrates: 20g

Protein: 5g

Stuffed Grape Leaves with Tzatziki Sauce

Prep Time: 20 minutes

Cook Time: (depends on grape leaves)

Servings: 4-6

Ingredients:

1 jar (16 oz) grape leaves, rinsed and drained

1 cup cooked brown rice

1/2 cup crumbled feta cheese

1/4 cup chopped fresh parsley

1 tablespoon chopped fresh mint

1 tablespoon olive oil

1 lemon, juiced

Salt and pepper to taste

For the Tzatziki Sauce:

1 cup plain Greek yogurt

1/2 cucumber, seeded and grated

1 tablespoon olive oil

1 clove garlic, minced

1/4 teaspoon dried dill

Salt and pepper to taste

Directions:

Prepare the filling: In a bowl, combine cooked brown rice, feta cheese, parsley, mint, olive oil, lemon juice, salt, and pepper. Mix well.

Assemble the grape leaves: Place a spoonful of the filling onto the wider end of a grape leaf. Roll up securely after folding the sides inward. Repeat with the remaining grape leaves and filling.

Cook the grape leaves: Follow the cooking instructions on the jar of grape leaves, which may involve simmering in water or broth.

Prepare the Tzatziki sauce: In a bowl, whisk together Greek yogurt, grated cucumber, olive oil, garlic, dill, salt, and pepper.

Tips:

Use pre-cooked brown rice for a quicker option.

Substitute chopped spinach or kale for the parsley and mint.

Serve the grape leaves warm or chilled, drizzled with Tzatziki sauce.

Nutritional Values (per serving with 2 grape leaves and Tzatziki sauce):

Calories: 250

Fat: 10g

Carbohydrates: 25g

Protein: 10g

Spiced Nuts and Seeds Mix

Prep Time: 10 minutes

Total Time: 10 minutes

Servings: 4-6

Ingredients:

1 cup raw almonds

1/2 cup raw cashews

1/4 cup pumpkin seeds

1/4 cup sunflower seeds

1 tablespoon olive oil

1/2 teaspoon ground cumin

1/4 teaspoon chili powder

1/4 teaspoon smoked paprika

Pinch of salt

Directions:

Preheat oven to 350°F (175°C).

Combine the nuts and seeds with the olive oil, cumin, smoked paprika, chili powder, and salt in a bowl.

Transfer the mixture onto a baking sheet and bake, stirring periodically, for 10 to 12 minutes, or until aromatic and golden brown.

Before serving, allow it cool somewhat.

Tips:

Use a variety of your favorite nuts and seeds like pecans, walnuts, or pepitas.

Adjust the spices to your preference. For a sweeter flavor, add a drizzle of honey or maple syrup.

Store the mix in an airtight container for up to a week.

Nutritional Values (per serving):

Calories: 200

Fat: 15g

Carbohydrates: 10g

Protein: 5g

Marinated Olives and Feta Cheese

Prep Time: 10 minutes

Total Time: 30 minutes (including marinating time)

Servings: 4-6

Ingredients:

1 cup pitted Kalamata olives

1/2 cup crumbled feta cheese

1/4 cup extra virgin olive oil

1 tablespoon lemon juice

1/2 teaspoon dried oregano

1/4 teaspoon garlic powder

Pinch of red pepper flakes (optional)

Directions:

Olives, feta cheese, lemon juice, olive oil, oregano, garlic powder, and red pepper flakes (if using) should all be combined in a bowl.

For a deeper flavor, marinate for at least 30 minutes or overnight after tossing to coat.

For easier consumption, serve with toothpicks.

Tips:

Use a variety of marinated olives like green olives or Castelvetrano olives for added flavor and texture.

Add chopped fresh herbs like parsley or thyme for extra freshness.

Serve with crackers or bread slices for a more complete appetizer.

Nutritional Values (per serving):

Calories: 250

Fat: 15g

Carbohydrates: 5g

Protein: 10g

Baked Sweet Potato Chips with Herbed Yogurt Dip

Prep Time: 15 minutes

Cook Time: 20-25 minutes

Servings: 2-3

Ingredients:

For the chips:

1 large sweet potato, thinly sliced

1 tablespoon olive oil

1/2 teaspoon salt

1/4 teaspoon black pepper

For the herbed yogurt dip:

1/2 cup plain Greek yogurt

1 tablespoon chopped fresh dill

1 tablespoon chopped fresh chives

1/4 teaspoon lemon juice

Pinch of salt and pepper

Directions:

Preheat oven to 400°F (200°C).

Line a baking sheet with parchment paper.

Add salt, pepper, and olive oil to sweet potato slices and toss.

Place the slices on the baking sheet that has been prepared in a single layer.

Bake, rotating halfway through, for 20 to 25 minutes, or until golden brown and crispy.

As the chips bake, get the dip ready.

Greek yogurt, dill, chives, lemon juice, salt, and pepper should all be combined in a small bowl.

Once fully combined, chill until ready to serve.

Tips:

Use a mandoline slicer for even and thin sweet potato slices.

Sprinkle the chips with your favorite spices like paprika, garlic powder, or cumin for additional flavor variations.

Serve the chips warm with the chilled yogurt dip for a delicious and satisfying snack.

Nutritional Values (per serving with chips and dip):

Calories: 300

Fat: 10g

Carbohydrates: 35g

Protein: 5g

CHAPTER SIX

Soup Recipes

Soups are a versatile and nourishing staple in the Atlantic Diet, offering a comforting and satisfying way to incorporate a variety of vegetables, lean protein, and healthy fats into your meals. They can be enjoyed as a light lunch, a hearty starter, or a warming main course.

Here are some key principles for Atlantic Diet soups:

Focus on fresh, seasonal ingredients: Utilize vegetables at their peak ripeness for optimal flavor and nutrient content.

Embrace broth-based soups: Opt for low-sodium vegetable or chicken broth as a base for added flavor and hydration.

Incorporate lean protein: Include sources like beans, lentils, fish, or chicken for increased satiety and nutrient diversity.

Healthy fats are your friend: Drizzle with olive oil or use avocado for creaminess without compromising nutritional benefits.

Now, dive into these delicious and nutritious soup recipes that embody the Atlantic Diet principles:

Classic Portuguese Caldo Verde Soup

Prep Time: 15 minutes

Cook Time: 30 minutes

Servings: 4-6

Ingredients:

4 tablespoons olive oil

1 medium onion, chopped

2 cloves garlic, minced

1 pound potatoes, peeled and diced

4 cups vegetable broth

1 bunch kale, ribs removed and thinly sliced

1/2 cup chopped smoked sausage (linguica or chourico)

Salt and pepper to taste

Directions:

In a big pot or Dutch oven, warm up the olive oil over medium heat.

Simmer the onion for approximately five minutes, or until it becomes tender.

Cook the garlic for one more minute, or until aromatic.

Add the veggie broth and potatoes and stir. Once the potatoes are soft, bring to a boil, then lower the heat and simmer for 15 minutes.

Add the smoked pork and greens. Cook the kale for a further five minutes, or until it has wilted.

Season with salt and pepper, to taste.

Warm up and serve with crusty bread (optional).

Tips:

Use kale or collard greens for the leafy greens.

Substitute other vegetables like carrots, turnips, or green beans for added variety.

For a vegetarian option, omit the smoked sausage.

Nutritional Values (per serving):

Calories: 300

Fat: 10g

Carbohydrates: 35g

Protein: 10g

Creamy Tomato and Red Pepper Soup

Prep Time: 10 minutes

Cook Time: 25 minutes

Servings: 4-6

Ingredients:

1 tablespoon olive oil

1 onion, chopped

2 cloves garlic, minced

2 red bell peppers, chopped

1 (28-ounce) can crushed tomatoes

4 cups vegetable broth

1/2 cup heavy cream (or unsweetened almond milk for a vegan option)

1 teaspoon dried basil

1/2 teaspoon dried oregano

Salt and pepper to taste

Directions:

In a big pot or Dutch oven, warm up the olive oil over medium heat.

Simmer the onion for approximately five minutes, or until it becomes tender.

Add the red peppers and garlic. Simmer for five more minutes, or until tender.

Add the oregano, basil, vegetable broth, and smashed tomatoes and stir. After bringing to a boil, lower the heat, and simmer for fifteen minutes.

Puree the soup with a blender or immersion blender until it's smooth.

Add heavy cream (or almond milk), stir, and fully cook.

Season with salt and pepper, to taste.

Serve hot with a garnish of fresh basil or parsley (optional).

Tips:

Roast the red peppers for added depth of flavor. Simply place them on a baking sheet, broil until slightly charred, and remove the skin before adding them to the soup.

Add a small pinch of red pepper flakes to make the soup hotter.

Serve with a dollop of Greek yogurt or a sprinkle of Parmesan cheese for extra richness.

Nutritional Values (per serving):

Calories: 250

Fat: 15g

Carbohydrates: 20g

Protein: 5g

Chilled Cucumber and Yogurt Soup

Prep Time: 10 minutes

Total Time: 2 hours (including chilling)

Servings: 4-6

Ingredients:

2 large cucumbers, peeled and chopped

1 cup plain Greek yogurt

1/2 cup chopped fresh dill

1/4 cup chopped fresh mint

1 tablespoon lemon juice

1 clove garlic, minced

1/4 cup water or vegetable broth (optional)

Salt and pepper to taste

Directions:

In a blender, combine cucumbers, yogurt, dill, mint, lemon juice, garlic, and water (if using).

Blend until smooth. Season with salt and pepper to taste.

To ensure it's cold, cover and chill for a minimum of two hours.

Serve cold, garnished with additional fresh herbs, chopped cucumber, or a drizzle of olive oil (optional).

Tips:

For a creamier soup, use full-fat Greek yogurt.

For a mild heat, add a small pinch of red pepper flakes.

Serve with crusty bread or crackers for dipping.

Nutritional Values (per serving):

Calories: 150

Fat: 5g

Carbohydrates: 15g

Protein: 5g

Italian Minestrone Soup

Prep Time: 15 minutes

Cook Time: 45 minutes

Servings: 6-8

Ingredients:

2 tablespoons olive oil

1 onion, chopped

2 carrots, chopped

2 celery stalks, chopped

2 cloves garlic, minced

1 (14.5 oz) can diced tomatoes, undrained

4 cups vegetable broth

1 cup small pasta (e.g., elbow macaroni, ditalini)

1 (15 oz) can cannellini beans, rinsed and drained

1 (15 oz) can kidney beans, rinsed and drained

1 cup frozen peas

1/2 cup chopped fresh basil

Salt and pepper to taste

Directions:

Heat the olive oil in a large pot or Dutch oven over medium heat.

Add onion, carrots, and celery. Simmer until tender, about 5 minutes.

Add the garlic and cook for a further minute, or until fragrant.

Stir in the pasta, diced tomatoes, and vegetable broth. Once it reaches a boil, reduce the heat and let it gently simmer for fifteen minutes.

Add the cannellini beans, kidney beans, and peas. Simmer for a further 10 minutes or so, or until pasta is cooked through and vegetables are tender.

After adding the basil, season with salt and pepper to taste.

Serve hot with crusty bread (optional).

Tips:

Use a variety of your favorite vegetables like zucchini, green beans, or corn.

For a heartier soup, add cooked shredded chicken or sausage.

Leftovers can be stored in the refrigerator for up to 3 days.

Nutritional Values (per serving):

Calories: 400

Fat: 10g

Carbohydrates: 50g

Protein: 15g

Clam Chowder with Fresh Herbs

Prep Time: 15 minutes

Cook Time: 30 minutes

Servings: 4-6

Ingredients:

2 tablespoons olive oil

1 onion, chopped

2 celery stalks, chopped

2 cloves garlic, minced

1 teaspoon dried thyme

1/2 teaspoon dried bay leaf

4 cups low-sodium chicken broth

1 (14.5 oz) can diced tomatoes, undrained

1 pound littleneck clams, scrubbed and rinsed

1/2 cup chopped fresh parsley

1/4 cup chopped fresh dill

1/4 cup heavy cream (or unsweetened almond milk for a vegan option)

Salt and pepper to taste

Directions:

In a big pot or Dutch oven, warm up the olive oil over medium heat.

Add the garlic, onion, and celery. Simmer for about 5 minutes, or until tender.

Add bay leaf and thyme and stir. Simmer one more minute, or until aromatic.

Add diced tomatoes and chicken broth. Heat till boiling.

Cook the clams for five to seven minutes, or until they open. Throw away any unopened clams.

Take out and dispose of the bay leaf.

Add dill, parsley, and heavy cream (or almond) and stir.

Add heavy cream (or almond milk) and parsley and dill and stir. To taste, add salt and pepper for seasoning.

Bring to a boil but do not boil.

Serve hot with crusty bread or oyster crackers (optional).

Tips:

Use fresh clams for the best flavor, but canned clams can be substituted for convenience.

For a richer chowder, add a roux made with butter and flour before adding the broth.

Experiment with different fresh herbs like tarragon or chives for added flavor variations.

Nutritional Values (per serving):

Calories: 350

Fat: 15g

Carbohydrates: 30g

Protein: 20g

CHAPTER SEVEN

Pasta and Grain Recipes

The Atlantic Diet incorporates whole grains and thoughtfully chosen pastas as a source of complex carbohydrates, fiber, and essential nutrients. This chapter offers a variety of delicious and satisfying recipes that showcase the versatility of these ingredients while adhering to the core principles of the diet.

Here are some key considerations for Atlantic Diet pasta and grain dishes:

Opt for whole grains: Choose whole-wheat pasta, brown rice, quinoa, barley, or farro for added fiber and nutrient content.

Portion control: Enjoy moderate serving sizes to avoid overconsumption of carbohydrates.

Pair with protein and vegetables: Include lean protein sources like fish, chicken, legumes, or tofu, and an abundance of vegetables for a balanced and filling meal.

Healthy fats are welcome: Drizzle with olive oil, use avocado, or incorporate nuts and seeds for healthy fats and added flavor.

Now, explore these flavorful and nutritious pasta and grain recipes that embody the Atlantic Diet principles:

Mediterranean Orzo Salad

Prep Time: 15 minutes

Total Time: 15 minutes

Servings: 4-6

Ingredients:

1 ½ cups dry orzo pasta

1 pint grape or cherry tomatoes, halved

2 green onions, with their white and green portions sliced and clipped

½ green bell pepper, seeds removed, chopped

1 cup packed chopped fresh parsley

½ cup packed chopped fresh dill

¼ cup sliced pitted Kalamata olives

2 teaspoons capers

1 tablespoon crumbled feta cheese (optional)

1 tablespoon olive oil

1 tablespoon lemon juice

¼ teaspoon dried oregano

Salt and pepper to taste

Directions:

Cook the orzo as directed on the package, then drain.

Cooked orzo, tomatoes, green onions, bell pepper, parsley, dill, olives, and capers should all be combined in a big bowl.

Mix the olive oil, lemon juice, oregano, salt, and pepper in a another bowl.

Drizzle the orzo mixture with the dressing, then toss to coat.

Serve with crumbled feta cheese on top, if using.

Tips:

Use chopped cucumbers, zucchini, or artichoke hearts for additional flavor and texture variations.

Serve the salad on a bed of romaine lettuce or spinach for a more complete meal.

Substitute crumbled goat cheese or vegan cheese alternatives for feta cheese.

Nutritional Values (per serving):

Calories: 300

Fat: 10g

Carbohydrates: 30g

Protein: 10g

Pesto Pasta with Cherry Tomatoes

Prep Time: 10 minutes

Cook Time: 15 minutes

Servings: 4

Ingredients:

12 ounces whole-wheat pasta (e.g., penne, fusilli)

1 cup cherry tomatoes, halved

½ cup prepared pesto

¼ cup chopped fresh basil

2 tablespoons grated Parmesan cheese

Salt and pepper to taste

Directions:

Pasta should be prepared as directed on the package, drained, and set aside with some pasta water.

Add a little olive oil and salt to the cherry tomatoes and mix while the pasta cooks. Bake at 400°F (200°C) for 10 to 12 minutes, or until the edges begin to blister and become somewhat softer.

Cooked pasta, roasted tomatoes, pesto, basil, and Parmesan cheese should all be combined in a big bowl.

Toss to coat; if necessary, add some of the leftover pasta water to get the right consistency.

Season with salt and pepper, to taste.

Tips:

Make your own pesto using fresh basil, pine nuts, garlic, olive oil, and Parmesan cheese.

Squeeze in some lemon juice for a more vibrant taste.

For a protein boost, stir in cooked chicken or shrimp.

Nutritional Values (per serving):

Calories: 450

Fat: 15g

Carbohydrates: 50g

Protein: 20g

Spaghetti Squash with Tomato Basil Sauce

Prep Time: 15 minutes

Cook Time: 40-45 minutes

Servings: 4

Ingredients:

1 medium spaghetti squash (4-5 pounds)

1 tablespoon olive oil

2 cloves garlic, minced

1 (14.5-ounce) can diced tomatoes, undrained

½ cup chopped fresh basil, divided

1/4 cup chopped fresh parsley

Salt and pepper to taste

Directions:

Preheat oven to 400°F (200°C).

Scoop out the seeds after cutting the spaghetti squash in half lengthwise. After seasoning with salt and pepper, drizzle the meat with olive oil.

Squash halves should be placed on a baking pan, cut-side down. Bake for 35 to 40 minutes, or until the food is fork-tender.

Meanwhile, place a skillet over medium heat with olive oil. Add the garlic and heat for 30 seconds or until fragrant.

Add chopped tomatoes and boil until slightly thickened, about 10 minutes.

Take off the burner and add half of the fresh basil. To taste, add salt and pepper for seasoning.

After the squash is cooked, scrape the flesh into spaghetti-like strands using a fork.

Evenly distribute the spaghetti squash among the dishes. Add tomato sauce over top and garnish with the remaining parsley and fresh basil.

Tips:

For a richer sauce, add a tablespoon of tomato paste along with the diced tomatoes.

Substitute other herbs like oregano or thyme for the basil.

Top with a sprinkle of grated Parmesan cheese or nutritional yeast for added flavor and protein.

Nutritional Values (per serving):

Calories: 250

Fat: 5g

Carbohydrates: 40g

Protein: 5g

Barley Risotto with Mushrooms and Parmesan

Prep Time: 15 minutes

Cook Time: 40 minutes

Servings: 4-6

Ingredients:

1 tablespoon olive oil

1 onion, chopped

2 cloves garlic, minced

1 cup pearl barley

4 cups vegetable broth

½ cup dry white wine (optional)

8 ounces sliced mushrooms

½ cup grated Parmesan cheese

2 tablespoons chopped fresh parsley

Salt and pepper to taste

Directions:

In a big pot or Dutch oven, warm up the olive oil over medium heat.

Simmer the onion for approximately five minutes, or until it becomes tender.

Add the garlic and simmer, stirring, for one more minute, or until fragrant.

Stir continually for a minute after adding the pearl barley and toasting it.

If using, add the white wine and heat until it evaporates, making sure to scrape away any browned bits from the pot's bottom.

Stir often and add ½ cup of vegetable broth at a time, letting the barley absorb the liquid before adding more.

When the barley is almost done, about 30 minutes, add the mushrooms and stir.

Simmer for a another five to ten minutes, or until the barley is creamy and soft and the mushrooms have softened.

Take off the heat and mix in the parsley and Parmesan cheese. To taste, add salt and pepper for seasoning.

Tips:

Substitute vegetable broth with chicken broth for added flavor.

Use other vegetables like peas, asparagus, or chopped spinach for additional variations.

For a vegan option, omit the Parmesan cheese and use a vegan cheese alternative.

Nutritional Values (per serving):

Calories: 350

Fat: 10g

Carbohydrates: 45g

Protein: 15g

Farro Salad with Roasted Vegetables

Prep Time: 15 minutes

Cook Time: 40 minutes

Servings: 4-6

Ingredients:

1 cup farro

1 tablespoon olive oil

1 red bell pepper, chopped

1 yellow bell pepper, chopped

1 zucchini, chopped

1 red onion, thinly sliced

½ cup crumbled feta cheese

¼ cup chopped fresh parsley

2 tablespoons lemon juice

1 tablespoon olive oil

Salt and pepper to taste

Directions:

Cook the farro as directed on the box, then drain.

Turn the oven on to 400°F, or 200°C.

Combine red onion, zucchini, and bell peppers with salt, pepper, and olive oil. After spreading out on a baking sheet, roast for 20 to 25 minutes, or until soft and beginning to turn golden brown.

Cooked farro, roasted veggies, feta cheese crumbles, and chopped parsley should all be combined in a big bowl.

Whisk together lemon juice, olive oil, salt, and pepper in a separate bowl.

Shake to coat the salad after adding the dressing.

Serve cold or room temperature.

Tips:

Use other seasonal vegetables like broccoli florets, cherry tomatoes, or asparagus for added variety.

Instead of farro, try brown rice or quinoa.

Drizzle the salad with a balsamic glaze for a sweeter flavor profile.

Nutritional Values (per serving):

Calories: 350

Fat: 15g

Carbohydrates: 40g

Protein: 10g

CHAPTER EIGHT

Seafood Recipes

Seafood plays a central role in the Atlantic Diet, providing a rich source of lean protein, healthy fats, and essential nutrients. This chapter features a variety of delicious and versatile seafood recipes that are both flavorful and heart-healthy.

Here are some key principles for incorporating seafood into the Atlantic Diet:

Choose sustainable options: Opt for seafood varieties that are abundant and responsibly sourced to ensure environmental sustainability.

Variety is key: Explore different types of fish and shellfish to benefit from a wider range of nutrients and flavors.

Cooking methods matter: Utilize healthy cooking methods like grilling, baking, pan-searing, and poaching to preserve nutrients and avoid excessive added fats.

Pair with healthy accompaniments: Complement your seafood dishes with whole grains, vegetables, and healthy fats for a balanced and satisfying meal.

Now, dive into these delectable and nutritious seafood recipes that embody the Atlantic Diet principles:

Grilled Swordfish with Lemon and Herbs

Prep Time: 10 minutes

Cook Time: 10-12 minutes

Servings: 4

Ingredients:

4 swordfish steaks (6-8 ounces each)

2 tablespoons olive oil

1 tablespoon lemon juice

1 teaspoon dried oregano

½ teaspoon garlic powder

¼ teaspoon salt

¼ teaspoon black pepper

Fresh herbs (optional): Chopped parsley, dill, or thyme

Directions:

Preheat grill to medium-high heat.

Olive oil, lemon juice, oregano, garlic powder, salt, and pepper should all be combined in a basin.

For a richer taste, marinate swordfish steaks in the marinade for up to 30 minutes, although at least 15 minutes is recommended.

After the fish has been removed from the marinade, discard the marinade.

Swordfish steaks should be cooked through and just beginning to flake after 4–5 minutes on each side of the grill.

Serve right away after adding an optional fresh herb garnish.

Tips:

Use a grill basket to prevent the fish from sticking to the grates.

If grilling indoors, use a grill pan or cast iron skillet.

Substitute other herbs like rosemary or basil for the oregano.

Nutritional Values (per serving):

Calories: 300

Fat: 15g

Carbohydrates: 0g

Protein: 35g

Pan-Seared Scallops with Citrus Salsa

Prep Time: 10 minutes

Cook Time: 5-7 minutes

Servings: 2

Ingredients:

12 large sea scallops

1 tablespoon olive oil

Salt and pepper to taste

For the Citrus Salsa:

¼ cup diced red onion

¼ cup chopped fresh cilantro

2 tablespoons chopped fresh orange or grapefruit

1 tablespoon lime juice

1 tablespoon olive oil

Pinch of salt

Directions:

Get the salsa ready: Mix the orange or grapefruit, red onion, cilantro, lime juice, olive oil, and salt in a bowl. Stir thoroughly and reserve.

Using paper towels, gently pat dry the scallops. Add pepper and salt for seasoning.

In a big skillet set over medium-high heat, warm up the olive oil.

Sear the scallops until they are cooked through and golden brown, 2 to 3 minutes per side.

Spoon the citrus salsa over the scallops and serve right away.

Tips:

Use dry sea scallops for optimal sear.

For a spicier salsa, add a pinch of red pepper flakes.

Serve the scallops over a bed of quinoa or rice for a more complete meal.

Nutritional Values (per serving):

Calories: 300

Fat: 15g

Carbohydrates: 5g

Protein: 20g

Baked Salmon with Dill and Lemon

Prep Time: 10 minutes

Cook Time: 15-20 minutes

Servings: 4

Ingredients:

4 salmon fillets (6-8 ounces each)

2 tablespoons olive oil

1 tablespoon lemon juice

1 teaspoon dried dill

½ teaspoon garlic powder

¼ teaspoon salt

¼ teaspoon black pepper

1 lemon, thinly sliced (optional)

Directions:

Preheat oven to 400°F (200°C).

Mix the olive oil, lemon juice, garlic powder, dill, salt, and pepper in a bowl.

Brush the salmon fillets with the marinade and place them on a baking dish.

Optionally, garnish the salmon with slices of lemon.

Bake the salmon for 15 to 20 minutes, or until it is cooked through and flake readily when tested with a fork.

Tips:

Use fresh dill for the most vibrant flavor.

Substitute other herbs like parsley or thyme for the dill.

For a well-balanced supper, serve with roasted veggies or a side salad.

Nutritional Values (per serving):

Calories: 400

Fat: 20g

Carbohydrates: 0g

Protein: 40g

Shrimp and Vegetable Stir-Fry

Prep Time: 10 minutes

Cook Time: 10-12 minutes

Servings: 4

Ingredients:

1 pound shrimp, peeled and deveined

1 tablespoon olive oil

1 red bell pepper, sliced

1 green bell pepper, sliced

1 broccoli floret, chopped

1 cup sugar snap peas

½ cup chopped onion

2 cloves garlic, minced

1 tablespoon soy sauce

1 tablespoon rice vinegar

1 teaspoon cornstarch

¼ cup water

Salt and pepper to taste

Directions:

Heat the olive oil in a big skillet or wok over medium-high heat.

Cook the shrimp for two to three minutes on each side, or until they are cooked through and pink. Take out of the pan and place aside.

To the pan, add the onion, bell peppers, broccoli, and sugar snap peas. Stir-fry for three to four minutes, or until starting to get soft.

Cook the garlic for one more minute, or until aromatic.

Mix the soy sauce, rice vinegar, cornstarch, and water in a small bowl.

After adding the sauce to the pan, simmer it. Cook for one to two minutes, or until slightly thickened.

Put the shrimp back in the pan and toss them around to coat in sauce.

To taste, add salt and pepper for seasoning.

Serve right away with noodles or rice.

Tips:

Use other vegetables of your choice, such as carrots, zucchini, or mushrooms.

For a thicker sauce, add an additional tablespoon of cornstarch mixed with water.

Serve with a sprinkle of sesame seeds or chopped peanuts for added flavor and texture.

Nutritional Values (per serving):

Calories: 400

Fat: 15g

Carbohydrates: 25g

Protein: 30g

Tuna Nicoise Salad

Prep Time: 15 minutes

Cook Time: 10 minutes (for hard-boiled eggs)

Servings: 4

Ingredients:

2 (12.5-ounce) cans tuna in water, drained and flaked

2 hard-boiled eggs, quartered

1 cup cherry tomatoes, halved

½ cup pitted Kalamata olives, halved

½ red onion, thinly sliced

2 green onions, sliced

1 cucumber, diced

¼ cup chopped fresh parsley

2 tablespoons olive oil

2 tablespoons lemon juice

1 tablespoon red wine vinegar

Salt and pepper to taste

Directions:

Boil the eggs if they aren't previously cooked. Place the eggs in a pot, cover with cold water, and bring to a boil. Switch off the heat source, cover, and let it sit for 12 minutes. After peeling, freeze under cold running water.

In a large bowl, mix together the flaked tuna, hard-boiled egg quarters, cherry tomatoes, olives, red and green onions, cucumber, and parsley.

In a separate bowl, combine the olive oil, lemon juice, red wine vinegar, salt, and pepper.

Pour the dressing over the salad and toss to coat.

Serve immediately over mixed greens or romaine lettuce.

Tips:

Use tuna in cans that has been packed in olive oil to add moisture and flavor.

For variation, try substituting different veggies like asparagus, green beans, or artichoke hearts.

Add quinoa or boiled potatoes for a heartier salad.

Nutritional Values (per serving):

Calories: 450

Fat: 20g

Carbohydrates: 20g

Protein: 30g

CHAPTER NINE

Vegetable Side Dish Recipes

Vegetables are a cornerstone of the Atlantic Diet, providing essential vitamins, minerals, fiber, and antioxidants. This chapter offers a variety of delicious and versatile vegetable side dish recipes that are both nutritious and flavorful.

Here are some key considerations for incorporating vegetables into the Atlantic Diet:

Variety is key: Explore a diverse range of vegetables in different colors and textures for a wider range of nutrients and to keep your meals interesting.

Seasonal choices: Opt for seasonal vegetables at their peak of freshness and flavor.

Healthy cooking methods: Utilize methods like roasting, grilling, steaming, and sauteing to preserve nutrients and enhance flavors.

Minimize added fats: Limit added oils and butter, and instead, use flavorful broths, herbs, and spices to season your vegetables.

Now, delve into these inspiring vegetable side dish recipes that perfectly complement your Atlantic Diet meals:

Roasted Garlic Cauliflower Mash

Prep Time: 10 minutes

Cook Time: 40-45 minutes

Servings: 4-6

Ingredients:

1 head cauliflower, cut into florets

2 tablespoons olive oil

1 head garlic, halved crosswise

Salt and pepper to taste

¼ cup unsweetened almond milk (or milk of choice)

1 tablespoon chopped fresh parsley (optional)

Directions:

Preheat oven to 400°F (200°C).

Toss the cauliflower florets with the olive oil, salt, and pepper. Spread out on a baking sheet and roast for 20 to 25 minutes, until starting to color and become tender.

While the cauliflower cooks, cut the garlic head in half, drizzle some olive oil on another piece of foil, and wrap it tightly. Next to the cauliflower, roast for 20 to 25 minutes, or until soft.

Once the garlic cloves have softened from roasting, take them out of their skins and transfer them to a basin.

Add the almond milk, roasted cauliflower, and salt & pepper to taste. Mash the potatoes with a masher or blend them in a food processor until the desired consistency is reached.

Garnish with the optional finely chopped fresh parsley and serve immediately.

Tips:

For a cheese taste, add a sprinkle of nutritional yeast.

Add some roasted sweet potato or red bell pepper to the cauliflower mash for a deeper flavor.

For up to three days, leftovers should be kept in the refrigerator in an airtight container.

Nutritional Values (per serving):

Calories: 150

Fat: 5g

Carbohydrates: 20g

Protein: 5g

Sauteed Green Beans with Almonds

Prep Time: 10 minutes

Cook Time: 10-12 minutes

Servings: 4

Ingredients:

1 pound fresh green beans, trimmed and cut into bite-sized pieces

1 tablespoon olive oil

1 shallot, thinly sliced

¼ cup sliced almonds

1 tablespoon lemon juice

Salt and pepper to taste

Directions:

The olive oil should be warmed in a large skillet over medium heat.

Saute the shallot for two to three minutes, or until it softens.

Boil the green beans for 5 to 7 minutes, stirring often, or until they are crisp-tender.

Stir the almonds in and cook for a further minute, stirring, until they become toasted and fragrant.

After adding the lemon juice, season with salt and pepper to taste.

Serve immediately.

Tips:

Use slivered almonds instead of sliced for a different texture.

Add a pinch of red pepper flakes for a touch of heat.

For a vegetarian protein boost, crumble cooked tofu or tempeh and add it to the pan with the almonds.

Nutritional Values (per serving):

Calories: 150

Fat: 10g

Carbohydrates: 10g

Protein: 5g

Balsamic Glazed Brussels Sprouts

Prep Time: 10 minutes

Cook Time: 20-25 minutes

Servings: 4

Ingredients:

1 pound Brussels sprouts, trimmed and halved

1 tablespoon olive oil

Salt and pepper to taste

¼ cup balsamic vinegar

1 tablespoon brown sugar

1 tablespoon Dijon mustard

Directions:

Preheat oven to 400°F (200°C).

Toss the Brussels sprouts with olive oil, salt, and pepper. Transfer to an oven tray and bake for 15 to 20 minutes, until starting to brown and become tender.

In a small saucepan, whisk together the brown sugar, balsamic vinegar, and Dijon mustard. Simmer for five to seven minutes, or until slightly thickened, over medium heat.

Once the Brussels sprouts are out of the oven, toss them with the balsamic glaze.

Return the Brussels sprouts to the oven and broil for an additional two to three minutes, or until the glaze is bubbling and caramelized.

Serve immediately.

Tips:

Before roasting, sprinkle chopped fresh herbs or bacon grease over the Brussels sprouts for extra flavor.

Replace the brown sugar with honey or maple syrup.

For a full dinner, serve the Brussels sprouts over brown rice or quinoa.

Nutritional Values (per serving):

Calories: 120

Fat: 5g

Carbohydrates: 15g

Protein: 3g

Grilled Asparagus with Lemon Zest

Prep Time: 5 minutes

Cook Time: 5-7 minutes

Servings: 4

Ingredients:

1 pound asparagus spears, trimmed

1 tablespoon olive oil

Salt and pepper to taste

1 lemon, zested

Directions:

Preheat grill to medium-high heat.

Toss asparagus spears with olive oil, salt, and pepper.

Grill the asparagus for 3-4 minutes per side, or until tender-crisp and slightly charred.

Remove from the grill and sprinkle with lemon zest before serving.

Tips:

To enhance the flavor of the asparagus, marinate it for 15 minutes in a mixture of olive oil, lemon juice, and garlic before grilling.

To keep the asparagus from drying out while grilling, wrap them with aluminum foil.

For even more flavor variations, drizzle some balsamic glaze or fresh lemon juice over the cooked asparagus.

Nutritional Values (per serving):

Calories: 50

Fat: 3g

Carbohydrates: 5g

Protein: 2g

Sauteed Swiss Chard with Garlic and Lemon

Prep Time: 10 minutes

Cook Time: 10-12 minutes

Servings: 4

Ingredients:

1 bunch Swiss chard, stems trimmed and chopped, leaves roughly chopped

1 tablespoon olive oil

2 cloves garlic, minced

¼ cup vegetable broth

1 tablespoon lemon juice

Salt and pepper to taste

Directions:

In a big skillet over medium heat, warm up the olive oil.

Add the garlic and sauté for 30 seconds, or until fragrant.

Sauté the Swiss chard stems for two to three minutes, or until they become soft.

Stir in the Swiss chard leaves and boil for an additional three to four minutes, or until the leaves wilt.

Once the lemon juice and vegetable broth have been added, scrape off any browned bits from the bottom of the pan.

Season with salt and pepper, to taste.

Simmer until the liquid has somewhat reduced, about 1 more minute.

Serve immediately.

Tips:

Add a pinch of red pepper flakes for a spicy kick.

Substitute kale or spinach for the Swiss chard.

Serve the Swiss chard with a sprinkle of grated Parmesan cheese or nutritional yeast for added flavor and protein.

Nutritional Values (per serving):

Calories: 70

Fat: 5g

Carbohydrates: 5g

Protein: 2g

CHAPTER TEN

Dessert Recipes

The Atlantic Diet encourages mindful indulgence, and sweet treats are no exception. This chapter offers a variety of delicious and satisfying dessert recipes that are mindful of sugar intake and incorporate wholesome ingredients.

Here are some key principles for incorporating desserts into the Atlantic Diet:

Focus on natural sweetness: Utilize fruits, honey, and maple syrup for natural sweetness instead of refined sugars.

Portion control: Enjoy desserts in moderation and savor smaller serving sizes.

Healthy fats: Include healthy fats like nuts, seeds, and avocados for added richness and satisfaction.

Mindful ingredients: Opt for whole grains, fruits, and yogurt as a base for your desserts.

Now, explore these delightful and nutritious dessert options that perfectly complement your Atlantic Diet lifestyle:

Fresh Fruit Salad with Honey Lime Dressing

Prep Time: 10 minutes

Total Time: 10 minutes

Servings: 4-6

Ingredients:

2 cups mixed berries (strawberries, blueberries, raspberries)

1 apple, diced

1 orange, segmented

½ cup sliced banana

¼ cup chopped pineapple

For the Honey Lime Dressing:

2 tablespoons fresh lime juice

1 tablespoon honey

1 teaspoon olive oil

Mint leaves for garnish (optional)

Directions:

In a large bowl, combine the mixed berries, apple, orange segments, banana, and pineapple.

In a separate bowl, whisk together lime juice, honey, and olive oil.

Pour the dressing over the fruit salad and toss gently to coat.

Garnish with mint leaves (optional) and serve immediately.

Tips:

Use seasonal fruits for added variety and freshness.

Substitute the honey with maple syrup for a different flavor profile.

For a creamier option, add a dollop of plain Greek yogurt to the dressing.

Nutritional Values (per serving):

Calories: 150

Fat: 3g

Carbohydrates: 25g

Protein: 2g

Greek Yogurt with Honey and Walnuts

Prep Time: 5 minutes

Total Time: 5 minutes

Servings: 1

Ingredients:

1 cup plain Greek yogurt

1 tablespoon honey

¼ cup chopped walnuts

A sprinkle of cinnamon (optional)

Directions:

In a bowl, combine Greek yogurt and honey.

Top with chopped walnuts and a sprinkle of cinnamon (optional).

Serve immediately.

Tips:

Use flavored Greek yogurt for a different taste variation.

Substitute chopped almonds, pecans, or granola for the walnuts.

Add a drizzle of almond butter or peanut butter for extra protein and healthy fats.

Nutritional Values (per serving):

Calories: 250

Fat: 10g

Carbohydrates: 20g

Protein: 15g

Orange and Almond Cake

Prep Time: 15 minutes

Cook Time: 40-45 minutes

Servings: 8-10

Ingredients:

1 cup whole wheat flour

½ cup almond flour

1 teaspoon baking powder

½ teaspoon baking soda

¼ teaspoon salt

½ cup unsalted butter, softened

½ cup honey

2 large eggs

1 teaspoon vanilla extract

Zest of 1 orange

½ cup freshly squeezed orange juice

¼ cup chopped almonds

Directions:

Preheat oven to 350°F (175°C). Grease and flour a loaf pan.

Mix the whole wheat flour, almond flour, baking soda, baking powder, and salt in a medium-sized basin.

Beat the butter and honey in a another basin until the mixture is light and creamy.

Add the orange zest and vanilla extract after beating in the eggs one at a time.

To the wet ingredients, alternately add the dry ingredients and orange juice, and stir just until mixed.

Add the chopped almonds and fold.

After filling the loaf pan with batter, bake it for 40 to 45 minutes, or until a toothpick inserted in the middle comes out clean.

After 10 minutes of cooling in the pan, move the food to a wire rack to finish cooling.

Tips:

For a richer flavor, substitute brown sugar for half of the honey.

Add a handful of chopped dried cranberries or raisins to the batter for additional sweetness and texture.

Dust the cooled cake with powdered sugar for a decorative touch.

Nutritional Values (per serving):

Calories: 300

Fat: 15g

Carbohydrates: 30g

Protein: 5g

Berry Compote with Vanilla Greek Yogurt

Prep Time: 10 minutes

Total Time: 10 minutes

Servings: 2

Ingredients:

1 cup mixed berries (strawberries, blueberries, raspberries)

2 tablespoons water

1 tablespoon honey

1 tablespoon lemon juice

1 cup plain Greek yogurt

¼ teaspoon vanilla extract

Directions:

In a small saucepan, combine berries, water, honey, and lemon juice.

Bring to a simmer over medium heat and cook for 5-7 minutes, or until the berries soften and release their juices.

Remove from heat and let cool slightly.

In a bowl, combine Greek yogurt and vanilla extract.

Spoon the berry compote over the yogurt and serve immediately.

Tips:

Use frozen berries for a quick and convenient option.

Substitute other fruits like peaches, cherries, or plums for the berries.

For a richer flavor, add a dollop of whipped cream or a sprinkle of granola to the top.

Nutritional Values (per serving):

Calories: 250

Fat: 5g

Carbohydrates: 30g

Protein: 15g

Chocolate Avocado Mousse

Prep Time: 10 minutes

Total Time: 10 minutes (plus chilling)

Servings: 2

Ingredients:

1 ripe avocado, peeled and pitted

½ cup unsweetened cocoa powder

2 tablespoons honey

1 tablespoon milk (dairy or non-dairy)

½ teaspoon vanilla extract

Pinch of salt

Directions:

In a food processor or blender, combine avocado, cocoa powder, honey, milk, vanilla extract, and salt.

Blend until smooth and creamy, scraping down the sides as needed.

Divide the mousse between two serving glasses and chill in the refrigerator for at least 30 minutes before serving.

Tips:

For a richer flavor, use dark chocolate cocoa powder.

Add a pinch of espresso powder for a deeper chocolate taste.

Top the mousse with fresh berries, chopped nuts, or a drizzle of honey for added garnish and texture.

Nutritional Values (per serving):

Calories: 300

Fat: 20g

Carbohydrates: 20g

Protein: 5g

Chapter Eleven

Beverage Recipes

Staying hydrated is crucial for overall health and well-being. This chapter features refreshing and flavorful beverage options that are aligned with the principles of the Atlantic Diet. These recipes are:

Low in added sugar: They minimize the use of processed sugars and artificial sweeteners, opting for natural sweetness from fruits and herbs.

Hydrating: They prioritize water-based beverages to keep you adequately hydrated throughout the day.

Nutrient-rich: They incorporate ingredients like fruits, vegetables, and spices that offer essential vitamins, minerals, and antioxidants.

Explore these delightful and healthy beverage options that perfectly complement your Atlantic Diet lifestyle:

Iced Green Tea with Mint

Prep Time: 5 minutes

Total Time: 15 minutes (including steeping)

Servings: 2

Ingredients:

2 green tea bags

1 cup boiling water

1 cup cold water

Fresh mint leaves, for garnish

Honey or maple syrup (optional, to taste)

Directions:

Steep the green tea bags in boiling water for 5 minutes.

Remove the tea bags and discard.

Stir in cold water and honey or maple syrup (optional) to taste.

Pour over ice and garnish with fresh mint leaves.

Tips:

For a stronger tea flavor, use loose leaf green tea instead of tea bags.

Add a squeeze of fresh lemon juice for a refreshing twist.

Substitute other herbs like basil or lemongrass for the mint.

Nutritional Values (per serving):

Calories: 5 (without sweetener)

Fat: 0g

Carbohydrates: 1g (with honey)

Protein: 0g

Citrus Infused Water

Prep Time: 5 minutes

Total Time: (including chilling)

Servings: Varies

Ingredients:

Water

Slices of your favorite citrus fruits (lemon, orange, grapefruit, etc.)

Optional additions: Sliced cucumber, berries, herbs like mint or basil

Directions:

Fill a pitcher or water bottle with water.

Add slices of your chosen citrus fruits and any additional flavorings.

Refrigerate for at least 30 minutes, or longer for stronger flavor.

Tips:

Experiment with different combinations of citrus fruits and herbs to create unique flavor profiles.

Muddle the fruits and herbs slightly before adding them to the water for a more intense flavor.

Use reusable water bottles to reduce waste and make this a sustainable beverage choice.

Nutritional Values (per serving):

Calories: 0

Fat: 0g

Carbohydrates: 0g

Protein: 0g

Smoothie with Spinach, Pineapple, and Coconut Water

Prep Time: 5 minutes

Total Time: 5 minutes

Servings: 1

Ingredients:

1 cup fresh spinach

1 cup chopped pineapple

½ cup coconut water

½ banana (optional)

¼ teaspoon ground ginger

Directions:

Combine all ingredients in a blender and blend until smooth and creamy.

Tips:

Use frozen pineapple for a thicker and colder smoothie.

Add a scoop of protein powder for an extra boost of nutrients.

Substitute other fruits like mango, berries, or papaya for the pineapple.

Nutritional Values (per serving):

Calories: 150

Fat: 2g

Carbohydrates: 25g

Protein: 2g (without protein powder)

Lemon Ginger Detox Drink

Prep Time: 5 minutes

Total Time: 5 minutes

Servings: 1

Ingredients:

1 cup warm water

1 lemon, juiced

1 inch fresh ginger, grated

Pinch of cayenne pepper (optional)

Honey or maple syrup (optional, to taste)

Directions:

Combine all ingredients in a mug and stir well.

Tips:

Adjust the amount of lemon juice and ginger to your taste preference.

For a more soothing drink, use lukewarm water instead of hot water.

This drink is not intended as a replacement for a balanced diet or medical advice.

Nutritional Values (per serving):

Calories: 5 (without sweetener)

Fat: 0g

Carbohydrates: 1g (with honey)

Protein: 0g

Turmeric Latte with Almond Milk

Prep Time: 5 minutes

Total Time: 5 minutes

Servings: 1

Ingredients:

1 cup unsweetened almond milk

1 teaspoon ground turmeric

½ teaspoon ground ginger

¼ teaspoon ground cinnamon

Pinch of black pepper

1 tablespoon honey or maple syrup (optional)

Directions:

In a small saucepan, heat almond milk over medium heat until simmering (do not boil).

Whisk in turmeric, ginger, cinnamon, and black pepper.

Remove from heat and stir in honey or maple syrup (optional) to taste.

Pour into a mug and enjoy warm.

Tips:

For a frothier latte, use a milk frother or whisk the heated milk vigorously before adding the spices.

Substitute other plant-based milk options like coconut milk or oat milk.

Add a pinch of cardamom or nutmeg for additional flavor variations.

Nutritional Values (per serving):

Calories: 70 (without sweetener)

Fat: 5g

Carbohydrates: 8g (with honey)

Protein: 1g

CHAPTER TWELVE

Conclusion

Congratulations on embarking on your journey with the Atlantic Diet! As you've explored these recipes and meal plans, you've gained valuable knowledge about incorporating delicious, nutritious foods into your daily routine.

Remember, the Atlantic Diet is not just about following a strict set of rules; it's about adopting a mindful and sustainable approach to eating. By focusing on whole, unprocessed foods, incorporating a variety of fruits and vegetables, and practicing mindful portion control, you can empower yourself to make informed choices that contribute to your overall well-being.

As you continue on this path, embrace the following takeaways:

Experiment and personalize: Don't be afraid to experiment with the recipes in this book and adapt them to your preferences and dietary needs.

Listen to your body: Pay attention to your hunger and fullness cues, and avoid restrictive eating patterns.

Enjoy the journey: Savor the process of preparing and eating healthy meals, and celebrate the positive changes you experience along the way.

The Atlantic Diet is not a destination, but rather a compass guiding you towards a healthier and more fulfilling relationship with food. By embracing its principles and incorporating them into your lifestyle, you can unlock a world of vibrant flavors, sustainable practices, and a renewed sense of well-being.

Printed in Great Britain
by Amazon